MINI-GUIDES

SOLDIERS IN NORMANDY: THE GERMANS...

June to August 1944

by Alexandre THERS

Lay-out by the author and Yann-Erwin ROBERT

Translated from the French by Jonathan NORTH

h&c
PRESS

GERMAN COMBAT CAPABILITY IN NORMANDY

In that slow Spring of 1944, France was a phony front for the Wehrmacht; it was a place where troops felt privileged to be sent to recuperate, reequip or to train. But the landings of June 6 were a rude shock as the Allies smashed into the German coastal divisions, most of which were untested in combat. Even so other divisions, based in Belgium or the Netherlands, were within reach and could influence the outcome of the campaign. In all, the divisions to hand numbered 738,047 men of which some 40,000 were placed on the Normandy frontline. What were the characteristics of these frontline divisions? What was their organization and their combat value? And what problems would they pose for the Allied expeditionary force?

Qualities and Faults

Coastal defenses in Normandy were part of the celebrated Atlantik Wall. Whilst a massive propaganda campaign vaunted this defensive system as being impregnable, replete as it was with coastal artillery, if the Wall was breached then the entire German line could collapse. Many of the German guns, particularly Flak batteries were static and immobile.

German units in Normandy on the eve of the invasion were as follows: the 77th, 91st, 243rd, 346th, 352nd, 709th, 711th and 716th infantry divisions of the German Army (Heer), the 17th Luftwaffe Field Division, 6th Fallschirmjäger Regiment, 21st Panzer Division and the 12th SS Panzer Division (Hitlerjugend). Those infantry divisions which were not motorized were roughly divided into classic divisions and static divisions, unable to maneuver. All of these divisions were something of a mixed bag, as the best German units were deployed on the Eastern Front, and many relied on horses for transportation.

The average age of the troops in Normandy varied considerably from division to division. The 352nd had troops aged around 18 to 19 whilst the 709th was made up of men around 36 years old. Similarly the presence of officers with combat experience also varied from unit to unit. In addition, the presence of some battalions of Ost Truppen, former prisoners of war taken from the Red Army and drafted into German service but of limited combat value, in some divisions, did not improve cohesion.

The one exceptional infantry unit was the 6th Fallschirmjäger Regiment, an elite unit of young soldiers, well-trained and motivated, they proved themselves formidable opponents.

Panzer divisions also experienced problems and shortcomings in the quality of the material they had to work with. These difficulties were exacerbated by a profound shortage of fuel. This was a crucial factor as it meant that fuel could not be wasted on training drivers or crews with the result that many of these key personnel had only a few hours of actual driving experience. Inexperience, even in battalions equipped with Panthers, led to accidents and losses. There were really only three armored divisions of sufficient quality to pose a threat on June 6: the Panzer Lehr, the 2nd Panzer Division and the 12th SS Panzer Division (Hitlerjugend). As with the fallschirmjagers, the SS divisions displayed astonishing morale and were extremely effective in combat. Although the Germans somehow convinced themselves that they were superior to the Allies this was pure theory. Indeed the Germans used equipment which was little better than that fielded by the Allies, with the possible exception of assault tanks and tank-destroyers, many of which were legendary. But any qualitative advantage was offset by Allied ability to replace losses (especially in tanks), by the wealth of supplies enjoyed by Allied soldiers, by the omnipresent reminder of Allied air superiority, and by artillery which played a tremendous role in enabling infantry victories.

Organization of German Divisions

It might be useful to take a look at a typical German formation. A Wehrmacht infantry division of 1944 comprised 12,769 men. It was based on three infantry regiments, each of two battalions, along with a battalion of reconnaissance troops (issued with bicycles). A battalion of anti-tank troops and a regiment of artillery, divided into three groups, made up the rest of the division. Depot cadres used to replace losses were included in the total but were only thrown into combat if the situation was really desperate. One of the most important units in the division was the anti-tank battalion and few divisions could do without them.

Heer and SS Panzer divisions had the same number of tanks, their effective strength being 101 Panzer IVs and 79 Panthers. A few had self-propelled guns in place of one of their tank battalions and these also might be used by some anti-tank battalions instead of Jagdpanzers and some units even had rockets. Some Heer or SS divisions fielded far fewer than their paper strength. The 77th Division was one of the worst off in terms of men and material having only 9,095 German troops plus 1,410 Eastern Volunteers when it went into action on June 20. In contrast the strongest division on June 6 was the Panzer Lehr Division which boasted more men in its ranks than it should theoretically have had. The 10th SS Panzer Division (Frundsberg) was in stark contrast again, having a single tank battalion but no anti-tank or assault guns. Even elite divisions such as the 1st SS Panzer Division (Leibstandarte Adolf Hitler) and the 2nd SS Panzer Division (Das Reich) lacked vehicles in which they could transport infantry. There again the Panzer Lehr had four battalions of infantry and could transport them all on a fleet of half-tracks.

The Context

The outcome of the struggle for Normandy was dictated by a number of key factors. Firstly, Allied air superiority over the Luftwaffe was a telling advantage especially when weather was good. The destruction wrought by Allied aircraft on communications lines, bridges and convoys, slowed down German movement and hampered the German intention of rapidly launching a series of counter-attacks. The psychological advantage of Allied air power also made itself felt on the morale of the German soldier.

Compared with the struggle in the East, the Normandy campaign was relatively small in terms of forces actually engaged. The concentration of overwhelming numbers at a single point was rendered difficult by the geographic limitations of the front and, in addition, the effects of the bocage have to be taken into account. Such terrain certainly favored troops on the defensive but it also posed problems as visibility was often obscured. In addition it was found extremely difficult to concentrate sufficient forces to counter enemy offensives. But in the bocage regions certain guerrilla tactics were found particularly useful and some German weaponry, including a varied arsenal of anti-tank weapons, came into its own.

On a tactical level it is often asserted that aggressive warfare is always more costly in human terms than defensive warfare but this was not always the case in Normandy. Losses depended on a certain number of factors including combat capability, manpower levels, quality of equipment, tactics, the application of surprise, topography in the combat zone, troop dispositions, firepower, air superiority, weather, supplies and ammunition, mobility and so on. One way of judging combat effectiveness is by analyzing a unit's ability to seize or hold terrain. In Normandy the Germans tried relatively infrequently to take back ground lost to the Allies. There was a counter-attack on July 11 at Dézert when the Panzer Lehr hit back. Despite a crushing numerical inferiority, the Germans pushed the Americans back a couple of miles and only called off the operation when overwhelming numbers came into the field against them. In the attacks around Mortain, the Germans had a two to one advantage in terms of men actually deployed at the outset. In addition they had more tanks but the Americans had the advantage in artillery. Even so it was something of an achievement that the Germans were able to advance five miles in the course of the operation.

Losses

In all some 640,000 German troops participated in the Normandy campaign. They suffered heavy losses (more men went missing than in a comparative sample of units engaged on the Eastern Front). Despite the number of troops encircled the relatively small number of troops taken prisoner shows that many German soldiers preferred not to surrender. Land operations cost the Germans 23,019 killed, 67,060 wounded and 198,616 missing. Some of the less reliable divisions showed a disproportionately high number of missing compared to sounder units which lost comparatively few in this regard. The greatest number of casualties was certainly suffered in the fighting in the Falaise pocket and, even for elite divisions, casualties here were heavy.

KRIEGSMARINE COASTAL GUNNER

The Germans established more than twenty large coastal batteries between Cherbourg and Le Havre and these were manned by Army and Navy personnel. In the course of the invasion these men were subjected to an onslaught from the air and from the sea.

Although the batteries, most of which were equipped with guns between 100 and 150mm caliber, would have to tackle an entire invasion fleet, not all were placed in protective casemates. But the batteries in Le Havre, and those at Bléville, had a range of 20 miles and those at La Hève 15 miles.

Most German batteries put up relatively feeble resistance on D-day and were soon silenced although the artillery position at Saint-Marcouf (Crisbecq) was something of an exception. This battery, on the eastern coast of the Cotentin peninsula, was served by a Kriegsmarine crew and they held out despite being bombarded by thousands of tons of bombs.

This photograph, and that on the opposite page, show a Kriegsmarine coastal gun crew on exercises. (© ECPAD/France)

A quartermaster 1st class belonging to a coastal battery. He wears a 1943 model fatigue cap and wears a telephone head set of the type used exclusively by gunners. He wears the 1933 grey-green uniform as issued in 1940-1942. The buttons bearing the anchor motif, the grey collar with yellow piping and the yellow eagle on his chest all denote his role. (Militaria Magazine)

6

In set: Coastal artillery badge. This was awarded to gunners who had acted bravely whilst under enemy fire. (Militaria Magazine)

Indeed, ably directed by their commander, Ensign 1st Class Walter Ohmsen, the gunners hit back and damaged a number of American ships. Shell-shocked and wounded, the Germans did not give up even when infantrymen belonging to the US 4th Infantry Division arrived on the scene and laid siege to the emplacements. Ohmsen even directed the Azeville batteries to open up on his own battery to drive the American infantrymen away. The garrison was finally pulled out on June 11 and Ohmsen was decorated with a Knights Cross for his achievements.

A shoulder strap belonging to a Kriegsmarine artillery NCO. (Bachmann Collection)

A hand-held siren. (Private collection)

The Merville battery, of particular strategic importance due to its position, was captured by British paratroopers after a particularly merciless struggle. The Mont Canisy battery, one of the most important German positions between Le Havre and Cherbourg, managed to sink a ship, badly damage 12 others and hit 22 more. The Longues-sur-Mer guns also fought valiantly. The battery had not yet been prepared for combat and was not completed by June 6. As no optical range-finders had been installed the German gunners had to engage targets with open-sights. The gunners pounded *HMS Bulolo*, the flagship of Commodore. Douglas-Pennant, Naval Commander for "Force G", the Gold Beach sector of the invasion fleet. Only when the French cruisers *Montcalm* and *Georges Leygues*, and the British *HMS Ajax*, appeared on the scene in the afternoon of June 6 did the situation alter.

German coastal guns often suffered from limited range and insufficient firepower. They were also beset by their isolation and this made it difficult for them to replenish their ammunition especially when the situation in the surrounding area was chaotic. Communication was also a problem and orders directing the batteries to open fire were sometimes never received because telephone lines had been cut.

The Grenadier

There were seven so called static divisions of German infantry manning coastal defenses in Normandy. They were the 243rd, 265th, 266th, 326th, 346th, 708th and 711th and they were a mixed bag of limited combat value and often without a full complement of troops.

This rather disheveled private is a veteran as can be seen by the fact that he wears an Iron Cross (2nd Class), the ribbon of which can be seen in his buttonhole, and a silver wounded award. (Militaria Magazine)

A Wehrpass, a book issued to all men of military age eligible for service in the German armed forces. (Militaria Magazine)

The average age of troops in these divisions varied considerably from one unit to another but was somewhere between 18 and 36 years. Similarly, the number of experienced officers also varied.

Most of these units knew only too well that they were there to plug the gap and their inadequate training, their inability to obtain adequate transportation and their inexperience all went towards creating poor morale. In just a few cases (the 265th and 266th for example) divisional commanders scraped together more mobile elements to create a Kampfgruppe.

The 243rd Division was sent to Normandy in the fall of 1943 and was posted to the north-west of the Cotentin peninsula around Portbail. It was gradually built up into a semi-mobile division reaching, in May 1944, standards applied to non-static divisions. Although up to strength it suffered very heavily in the fighting and, by the end of July, had ceased to exist as a fighting formation. The remaining troops found themselves encircled in Cherbourg. The 265th Division was stationed in Brittany but sent a Kampfgruppe into Normandy in response to D-day. It reached the front around Saint-Lô on June 11. Throughout *Operation Cobra* it fought alongside the 91st Division. It was eventually broken up and shared out among surviving units. The 266th also supplied a Kampfgruppe but this only reached the frontlines on June 23 and its relics were absorbed by the 352nd Division in early August.

The 326th was initially based in the Pas-de-Calais but was engaged piecemeal in Normandy from the end of July. By August it had been pushed

Top: A cover for the Linneman shovel as issued late on in the war. This tool was issued to all German soldiers. (Militaria Magazine)

A 1930 model gas mask. Poison gas was not actually used during the war but this piece of equipment was carried just in case. (Private collection)

Normandy in 1944 and a group of German infantrymen take a break. (© ECPAD/France)

back eastwards. The 346th had been based around Le Havre from the end of January 1944.

It lurched into life on June 6, attacking British positions around Bavent-Breville on the next day before switching to containing the bridgehead over the Orne.

From June 19 to mid-July its sector was relatively calm. During Operation Goodwood it managed to hold on to Troarn despite losing most of its infantry and 70% of its artillery. From August 9, it was pushed back steadily towards Falaise, managed to extricate itself from the pocket and crossed the Seine near Lisieux. The 708th had been brought up from the Bay of Biscay, arriving at the front on July 4 and establishing itself between Laval and Angers. Elements of the division which fought at Le Mans were destroyed.

The 711th was deploying to the east of the Orne when the Allies landed. Its sector was largely defended by the 346th Division and so the 711th played a marginal role in the defense.

This infantry private is a perfect example of how German soldiers appeared in 1944. He wears the late model green uniform, made out of poor quality cloth, which makes his uniform baggy. This is accentuated by the puttees which are far less martial than the traditional boots usually worn. (Militaria Magazine)

THE TANK CREWMAN

Along with the Waffen SS Panzer divisions the Army's Panzer divisions (of which there were five in Normandy — the 2nd, 9th, 21st, 116th and Panzer-Lehr) played a crucial part in any battle.

The 2nd Panzer Division had been stationed near Amiens at the time of the Allied landings. It was up to strength and boasted its full complement of equipment and vehicles. Its vanguard went into action on June 12 in the zones around Sées and Alençon.

After June 20 the bulk of the divisions operated around Caumont although *Operation Epsom* forced one of the division's battalions to redeploy against the British. On June 28 this battalion was credited with the destruction of 53 tanks and 12 anti-tank guns. The division also participated in the Mortain attack.

The 9th Panzer Division was surprised in the middle of being refitted and for that reason was in no fit state to take to the roads before July 27. A few elements went into action to the east of Domfront on August 4 and others fought to the west of Alençon and in the area around Trun but, on the whole, it made little impact. On August 6 a good part of the division went into action between Domfront and Mayenne, north of Montsûrs in the Alençon sector. The division escaped from the Falaise trap.

The 21st Panzer Division was in part distinguished by the vast quantity of vehicles it seemed to have at its disposal, many of them being French vehicles seized in 1940. The division fought around Caen in June and July before transferring northwards. It was one of the most roughly handled German units in the fighting.

The 116th Division was also up to strength and was held in reserve to the south-east of Caen until the Ameri-

This tank crewman has managed to escape from Normandy. In all 30,000 vehicles and 135 tanks managed to make it over the Seine. (© ECPAD/France)

An Army tank crewman's collar. (Private collection)

Right: A Tiger tank crew gathered around their heavy tank. There were just three battalions of heavy tanks in Normandy, one of which was an Army unit (s. Pz. Abt. 503). In all 126 such tanks were sent to Normandy. (© ECPAD/France)

Right: A 75mm explosive shell (KwK 40), ammunition used by Panzer IV types F2 and G. (Private collection)

These tankers are equipped in varying styles all popular among tank crews. The young officer on the left, however, wears a paratrooper's tunic with tank-crew collar tabs stitched on.
(© ECPAD/France)

A tank crewman's badge. These were awarded for participation in assaults covering three different days. (Private collection)

cans broke through to the west of Saint-Lô. Then, on July 28, it was directed towards Vire. At that time the division's battalions were up to strength and were mobile. In the course of the Mortain counter-attack one of its companies even got as far as Mesnil-Adelée. On August 11 the division was transferred to the Alençon-Argentan sector but it managed to escape the Falaise encirclement. When the Panzer-Lehr Division entered Normandy it was probably the best equipped of all the German divisions. Initially stationed around Chartres, Le Mans and Orléans it received orders on June 6 to head into Normandy. Its Panther battalion went into action against the British on June 11.

A month later, the division was back in the thick of the fighting, this time against the Americans around Dézert. Significantly weakened, it remained to the north-west of Saint-Lô. It suffered still further when *Operation Cobra* was launched and combat-worthy elements were pulled back to Argentan to reorganize.

This tank crewman wears protective overall over his regulation black uniform.
(Militaria Magazine)

11

THE KRIEGSMARINE SAILOR

The Germany Navy had some 140 surface warships and a few U-Boats in Normandy ports but these were too few to oppose the Allied armada.

If the U-Boats, destroyers and torpedo boats posed a threat to Allied shipping they were, in fact, just a small part of a German fleet which consisted in the main of mine-sweepers, armed trawlers, patrol boats and motor boats. Some 76 German vessels were at Le Havre, 15 were at Cherbourg and the rest distributed between Fécamp, Dieppe, Ouistreham and in the Channel Islands.

The sheer scale of the Allied invasion meant that a German naval response was never going to be truly effective. At dawn on June 6 three vessels (T28, *Jaguar*, *Falke* and *Möwe*) belonging to the 5th Torpedo Flotilla and commanded by Captain Heinrich Hoffmann found themselves face to face with the Allied invasion fleet. Despite the overwhelming disparity of forces, the Germans attacked and came under fire from the cruisers *HMS Warspite* and *HMS Ramillies*.

An S-Boote in a French port just before the Allied landings. From June 12th five flotillas of such craft operated in the West. They had six boats at Ostend, five at Boulogne, four at Cherbourg and 15 at Le Havre. (Bundesarchiv)

This sailor was part of a crew manning one of the Kriegsmarine's surface warships but the vessel has evidently been destroyed and he is now kitted out for operations on dry land. He wears the traditional double-breasted tunic and linen overall trousers. (Militaria Magazine)

A cap badge belonging to a Kriegsmarine mine-sweeping unit based in Normandy. (B. Malvaux collection)

Top: The crew of a Hilfsminensuchboot. (©)ECPAD/France)

The Germans launched 18 torpedoes but only the Norwegian destroyer *HNoMS Svenner* was sent to the bottom. The German ships, sending up a smoke screen pulled back to base not having suffered any casualties.

There were further actions against Allied shipping in the coming weeks, the 4th, 5th, 7th, 8th and 9th S-Boat Flotillas coming into play.

The Germans met with some success on June 7 when they sank an LST and a British LCI. The following day it was the Americans who fell victim to a German attack when they suffered the loss of two LSTs around midnight and the *USS Meredith* was also damaged.

On June 11 the frigate *HMS Halstead* was hit by a torpedo in the prow whilst the *USS Partridge* was also hit and went down in a matter of moments. Shortly afterwards a British tug, the *Sesame*, suffered the same fate whilst another LST was heavily damaged.

On June 12, a munitions transporter, the *Dungrange* and the British steamers *the Ashanti* and *Brackenfield* were hit off Juno Beach whilst the American destroyer *USS Nelson* was badly damaged.

So it was that, despite the overwhelming Allied advantage in numbers, the Kriegsmarine did manage to hit back at the Allied armada.

Sailors loading a torpedo. (© ECPAD/France)

Left: A Kriegsmarine wrist watch manufactured by Marton (bearing the mark Siegerin on the watch face). Other watches in use were made by Berg and Junghaus. (Private Collection)

13

THE WAFFEN-SS TANK CREWMAN

With five armored divisions and one division of Panzergrenadiers engaged in Normandy, the Waffen SS was the German military's trump card. With their superb tanks they outclassed most of the Allied armor arrayed against them. They were the bogeymen of the Anglo-American forces and the Allies tried their uppermost to destroy their combat potential.

An Iron Cross, 2nd Class. The different classes of the order were issued for varying degrees of courage shown before the enemy. (Militaria Magazine)

A laryngophone adapted for use onboard tanks. This allowed vocal commands to be transmitted as it picked up vibrations from the voice box. (Van Onsem collection)

A model of a Tiger tank. These tanks formed three battalions in Normandy, two of which belonged to the Waffen SS. (Charbonneau collection)

The Waffen SS divisions in Normandy were the 1st SS Panzer Division (Leibstandarte SS-Adolf Hitler), the 2nd SS Panzer Division (Das Reich), the 9th SS Panzer Division (Hohenstaufen), the 10th SS Panzer Division (Frundsberg), the 12th SS Panzer Division (Hitlerjugend) and the 17th SS-Frv. Panzergrenadier Division (Götz von Berlichingen).

The **Leibstandarte** was in the process of being rebuilt and was not combat ready. Only on June 17 could some of its first echelons begin the journey to Normandy. Most of the 1st SS Panzer Grenadier Regiment fought along Route Nationale 175 on the eastern flank of the British Epsom offensive. The bulk of the division was engaged by July 6. The Leibstandarte was being held in reserve to the south of Caen when the British launched *Operation Goodwood*. It was still there on the night of August 5 when elements were detached so that they could participate in the Mortain counter-attack. The division was one of those trapped in the Falaise pocket.

Das Reich lacked vehicles and equipment, and was insufficiently trained, when on the morning of June 7 it received the order to move out. It arrived in Domfront on June 13 and, on June 16, elements of the division had concentrated near Mortain. It was only fed into the frontline slowly towards the end of June. The division was one of the

Top: this tanker belongs to the 102d SS heavy tank (Tiger) battalion, fighting in July near the Odon river. He stands in the turret of a captured British scout car. (Bundesarchiv)

This Tiger belongs to the 102nd SS Battalion of Heavy Tanks. The number of air raids, the destruction of bridges, the lack of fuel and the bocage terrain all slowed the tanks down. (Bundesarchiv)

few to be sent against the Americans in July. Right until the end it was counter-attacking, showing considerable prowess in attempting to release trapped troops from the Falaise pocket.

Hohenstaufen took part in an attempt to stem *Operation Epsom* and achieved lasting fame on July 18 when it destroyed 67 Allied tanks. It remained in the sector to the south-west of Caen until early August when it was dispatched to Vire. On August 16, in combination with the Das Reich Division, it launched a counter-attack hoping to break the Falaise encirclement. Even by the end of August the division was still in relatively good condition.

Frundsberg was very poorly off in terms of equipment and vehicles. By June 25 most of the division had reached its assembly points. In the course of the following days the division went into line around Saint-Remy, Roucamps, La Bigne, Saint-Symphorien, Les Buttes, Campeaux, Vire and Tinchebray. The first action it saw was when it was deployed to counter the Allied *Operation Epsom* in July during which it was positioned to the south-west of Caen. From there it was also sent to Vire to the south of the salient ringing the German units near Falaise. Part of the division was encircled in that pocket.

Hitlerjugend was a relatively large division at the time of the Allied landing and was engaged on June 7 when its 25th SS Panzergrenadier Regiment, supported by tanks belonging to the II. SS Panzer Regiment 12, counter-attacked Canadian troops to the north of Caen. The division remained around Caen for the rest of the campaign. In August it fought a number of rearguard actions to cover the German withdrawal.

This NCO wears the camouflage overalls issued specifically to tank crews in 1944. This guaranteed the men some cover when outside of their tank. (Militaria Magazine)

15

THE PANZERGRENADIER

The Panzergrenadier, literally translated as "armored grenadier" was the name given to those infantrymen tasked with accompanying Germany's tanks. There were motorized and mechanized regiments.

Those belonging to the 2nd Panzer Division were almost entirely mechanized and made use of a number of half-tracks. Forward elements, carried forward on trucks, reached Sées-Alençon on June 11 and went into action the following day. The 9th Panzer Division's vanguard, on the other hand, belonged to a unit which was caught in the process of regrouping and only reached the front to the east of Domfront, west of Alençon and near Trun, on August 4. Other elements only managed to rally to the division after the destruction of the bridges over the Loire. But on August 6 the division went into action along the Domfront-Mayenne line, just to the north of Montsûrs in the Alençon sector.

The 125th and 192nd Panzergrenadier Regiments, belonging to the 21st Panzer Division, also had battalions which used half-tracks. The division fought in the Caen sector in June and July and went on to fight in the salient to the north of the city despite suffering heavy casualties. The bulk of the 116th Panzer Division, which included the 60th and 156th Panzergrenadier Regiments, reached its jumping off points on July 24. The division was, however, kept in reserve to the south-east of Caen but was orde-

A 1939 Model hand grenade. (Militaria Magazine)

An armored unit's combat badge in its bronze version. This was designed to reward Panzergrenadiers and machine gunners. (Militaria Magazine)

British paratroopers belonging to the 6th Airborne Division have been captured and are being escorted through Saint-Pierre-sur-Dives during the afternoon of June 6. Some Panzergrenadiers, including the men shown here, part of the 21st Panzer Division, preferred to wear camouflage. (© ECPAD/France)

Bayonets which were used with the German infantry's standard rifle — the Mauser 98k.

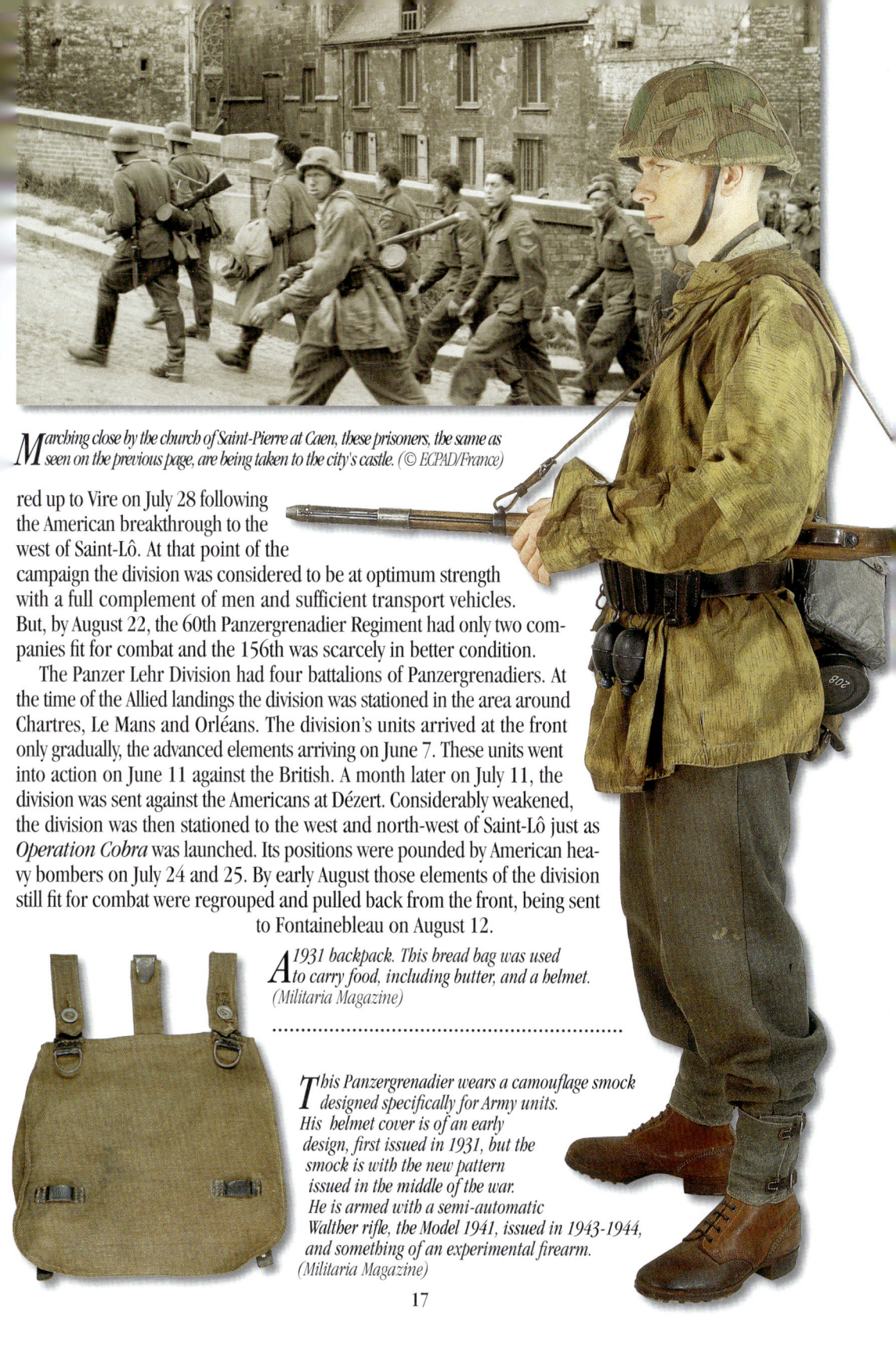

Marching close by the church of Saint-Pierre at Caen, these prisoners, the same as seen on the previous page, are being taken to the city's castle. (© ECPAD/France)

red up to Vire on July 28 following the American breakthrough to the west of Saint-Lô. At that point of the campaign the division was considered to be at optimum strength with a full complement of men and sufficient transport vehicles. But, by August 22, the 60th Panzergrenadier Regiment had only two companies fit for combat and the 156th was scarcely in better condition.

The Panzer Lehr Division had four battalions of Panzergrenadiers. At the time of the Allied landings the division was stationed in the area around Chartres, Le Mans and Orléans. The division's units arrived at the front only gradually, the advanced elements arriving on June 7. These units went into action on June 11 against the British. A month later on July 11, the division was sent against the Americans at Dézert. Considerably weakened, the division was then stationed to the west and north-west of Saint-Lô just as *Operation Cobra* was launched. Its positions were pounded by American heavy bombers on July 24 and 25. By early August those elements of the division still fit for combat were regrouped and pulled back from the front, being sent to Fontainebleau on August 12.

A 1931 backpack. This bread bag was used to carry food, including butter, and a helmet. (Militaria Magazine)

This Panzergrenadier wears a camouflage smock designed specifically for Army units. His helmet cover is of an early design, first issued in 1931, but the smock is with the new pattern issued in the middle of the war. He is armed with a semi-automatic Walther rifle, the Model 1941, issued in 1943-1944, and something of an experimental firearm. (Militaria Magazine)

THE ARTILLERYMAN

German artillery was potent but was unable to concentrate as much fire as that its adversaries could bring to bear. The German use of much captured equipment meant that their artillery had a vast range of calibers, rendering an adequate supply of ammunition problematic.

The Germans attempted to overcome this difficult situation by selecting guns from the disparate sources available to them and concentrating pieces together by type. Even so it was frequently the case that once a German battery commander

A Panzer Artillery regiment was composed of three battalions, the first equipped with 16 Wespe self-propelled guns and eight Hummels. The second had three batteries of 18 105mm cannon whilst the third had 12 155mm cannon and 4 100mm cannon. Only 17 independent artillery groups took part in the campaign amongst which was one long-range battery. (© ECPAD/France)

This senior artillery corporal uses a portable range-finder used to gauge distances for the precise firing of artillery. He has used tent canvas to fashion a camouflaged shirt for himself. (Militaria Magazine)

The Germans made use of one kind of weapon completely new to the Anglo-Americans — the Nebelwerfer rocket launchers. These were grouped into independent brigades (with the exception of three battalions assigned to the 1st and 12th SS Panzer Divisions and the 21st Panzer Division). Their presence effectively doubled the amount of German artillery which did not belong to individual divisions. But they had poor range and the fact that they consumed a massive amount of ammunition made resupply very difficult. (Bundesarchiv)

This badge, created on October 23, 1942, was awarded to drivers — including those of self-propelled guns, who had shown particular merit. (Private collection)

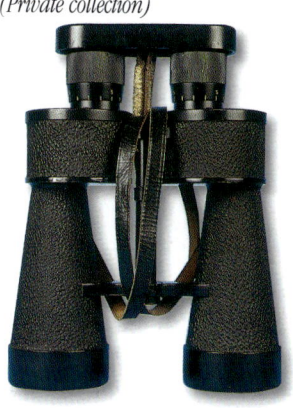

Binoculars 10x50. Such powered optical instruments were manufactured by firms like Leitz or Zeiss. (Militaria Magazine)

A regulation boot, issued in the standard brown leather and based on the 1901 model boot used throughout the First World War. From 1941 on it was also issued to gunners in an attempt to save on the use of leather. (Militaria Magazine)

ran out of ammunition he would have to order the spiking of his guns. But the main problem was that the German artillery arm suffered from deficiencies in organization. Most German artillery was assigned to particular divisions, meaning that it was employed, by and large, on localized tactical missions, making it difficult to concentrate pieces for large-scale actions. It also proved difficult for the Germans to introduce the relatively sophisticated system of concentrating sufficient guns under a single command.

In general, German artillery was also hampered by its inability to see long distances, being largely deprived of aerial reconnaissance or observation units. Worse was the fact that most munitions replenishment depended on horse-drawn transportation making the resulting slow-moving columns vulnerable to enemy artillery or air raids. So it was that German batteries, themselves largely immobile, suffered greatly from a real lack of ammunition. A brief examination of two German artillery units might give some indication as to the overall situation. On May 1, field artillery attached to the 716th Division consisted in part of captured Czech and French weapons, including 40 100mm and 155mm howitzers (excluding anti-tank weapons). The 352nd Division had 36 105mm howitzers and eight of 150mm on the same date. In addition to artillery assigned to particular divisions there were also a number of independent groups assigned to the general artillery reserve.

For example the SS Artillerie Abteilung 101, Artillerie Abteilung 456, 457, 460, 555, 628, 763, 989, 992, 1151, 1192, 1193, 1194, 1198, Artillerie Battery 625, Artillerie Schule Suippes and Artillerie Schule Autun, Werfer-Brigade 7, 8, 9, Steilungs-Werfer-Regiment 101 and SS Werfer-Abteilung 102 all fought in Normandy.

THE FALLSCHIRMJÄGER

Paratroopers were considered elite units among the infantry. Although officially part of the air force, they were, in effect, under Army command. The way in which the men were recruited, trained and equipped meant that their status was somewhat akin to that enjoyed by the Waffen SS.

Throughout the campaign the paratroopers wore their distinctive helmet covers or, if these were lacking, painted their helmets with camouflage paint. ((c)ECPAD/France)

A shoulder patch as worn by a Luftwaffe lieutenant. The yellow color was distinctive to navigators and paratroopers. (Militaria Magazine)

Right: A pocket knife of the type issued to Luftwaffe personnel. It was used, among other things, for cutting parachute cords after landing. Paratroop units in Normandy did not make any jumps during the campaign. (JLF collection)

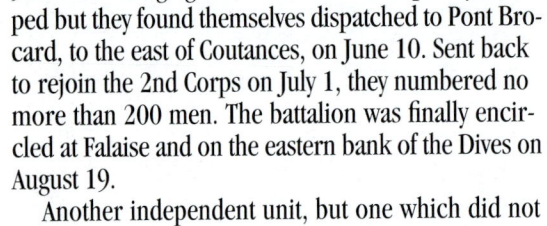

Right: Bourgtheroulde on August 25 or 26 1944. The retreat over the Seine was conducted in relatively good order. The losses suffered by the 3rd Division are estimated at around 11,000 men and those of the 5th at around 8,000. (© ECPAD/France)

The two most important units of paratroopers to see action in Normandy were the 3rd and 5th Fallschirm Divisionen. The 3rd assembled around Saint-Lô, although a combat group took up a position near Brécey and Villedieu on June 10th. This group was only semi-mobile and lacked artillery and was almost destroyed early on in the campaign. The 5th, which was extremely weak at this stage due to heavy losses in preceding campaigns, also lacked artillery. Its forward elements reached the Saint-Lô front on June 25 before making for Percy. Those elements following on were directed to the south-east of Avranches and to Villedieu, Lamballe and Dinan. Once again losses were very heavy.

In addition a brigade and two battalions of independent assault guns, belonging to the 2nd Fallschirm Corps, were also dispatched to Normandy. These were the Fallschirm-Sturmgeschütz-Brigade 12, the Fallschirm-Flak Abteilung 2 and the Fallschirm-Flak-Aufklärungs-Abteilung 12. The 900 men belonging to this latter unit were poorly trained and under-equipped but they found themselves dispatched to Pont Brocard, to the east of Coutances, on June 10. Sent back to rejoin the 2nd Corps on July 1, they numbered no more than 200 men. The battalion was finally encircled at Falaise and on the eastern bank of the Dives on August 19.

Another independent unit, but one which did not

Paratroopers belonging to the 2nd Division are here training in Brittany. One of the regiments forming the 2nd Division, the 6th, fought in Normandy. (J-Y Nasse collection)

originate from 2nd Corps, was the 6th Fallschirmjäger Regiment which was originally intended to reinforce the 2nd Fallschirm Division then regrouping in France. On June 6th it saw action in the sector around Lessay, Carentan and La Haye-des-Puits. That afternoon the German paratroopers attacked their American counterparts, men belonging to the 101st Airborne Division, around Carentan. They pushed into Vierville, heading for Brucheville where, after heavy fighting, they were repulsed. Those who lived to fight another day distinguished themselves in July, again in the vicinity of Carentan, so much so that they were nicknamed the Lions of Carentan. During *Operation Cobra* the unit was almost encircled at Villedieu and had to be pulled back. From August 10, the survivors tried to regroup at Nancy. One combat group attempted to stem the American advance at L'Aigle-Moulins on August 12.

Below: This anti-tank mine is of the kind used by paratroopers. A 4.5 kilogram charge was used. (Private collection)

This young paratrooper wears a jumpsuit of the kind issued in 1943. This was standard issue to paratroop units. (Militaria Magazine)

21

THE TANK KILLERS

German "tank busters" were soldiers armed with hand-held anti-tank weapons, most notably the redoubtable Panzerfaust and the Panzerschreck with its hollow charge. Difficult to spot, and capable of firing through hedges or camouflaging themselves according to the terrain, these brave men were capable of delivering a mortal blow to many Allied tanks.

The tank busters were equipped with hand-held weapons and had the appearance of guerrilla fighters. They acted alone or in small groups spread thinly along a defensive perimeter. The Panzerfaust operator knew that the range of his weapon was relatively poor (between 40 and 70 yards according to the version in use) and that if he stood any change of success he had to get really close to his target. For that reason, good aim was not particularly important. The projectile fired from a Panzerfaust could penetrate armor up to six-inches thick. The operator knew that he had one chance to hit the target before beating a hasty retreat or facing annihilation. This redoubtable, and reliable, weapon could knock out most tanks.

The Panzerschreck, the German equivalent to the American Bazooka, had a range of more than 170 yards ad could penetrate seven inches of

This adjutant, an instructor, demonstrates the use of a Panzerfaust 30. (Bundesarchiv)

A stripe worn on the sleeve to denote a tank destroyed. It was issued for every such victory. (Militaria Magazine)

Above: The Panzerknacker or tank buster was a booklet issued on May 13 1944. It described the different techniques which might be used to destroy tanks at close range. (Militaria Magazine)

German infantrymen stop by at a Normandy farm. The young soldier in the foreground carries Panzerschreck missiles. More than 289,151 examples of this weapon were manufactured. (Bundesarchiv)

A German infantry column passes through a village in the Calvados region. A Panzerschreck and a Panzerfaust are evident here. (Bundesarchiv)

Top: The head of a Panzerfaust 60 projectile. (Militaria Magazine)

armor. Panzerschreck operators usually went to ground and from concealed positions could knock one tank out after another, particularly if they shot at the lower part of the hull where the armor was thin.

The tank busters cost the Allies heavy casualties and the liberators had tremendous problems rooting out these invisible assailants as the application of air power or artillery firepower was of little use in the bocage. The Germans were also too fleet of foot to be identified and dealt with by such methods. Panzerfausts and Panzerschrecks were by far the most typical hand-held anti-tank weapons but the Germans did employ other methods including bundles of grenades — in which six grenades were bound to a stick-grenade —, the Tellermine anti-tank mine and the magnetic 3-kilogramme charge.

An anti-tank magnetic charge. It could pierce six inches of armor. Developed so that it could be attached to tank superstructures it was actually a tricky weapon to use as it exploded just 7.5 seconds after being attached. Although superseded by the Panzerfaust, which was easier to use, this weapon was used in small numbers in Normandy. (Private collection)

This young tank destroyer carries a Panzerschreck, along with one of its projectiles, and also has a Panzerfaust 30. (Militaria Magazine)

23

THE WAFFEN SS PANZERGRENADIER

The Waffen SS was a military force in its own right and did not fall under Army command. Its recruitment, along with the way it instructed its members, was based on strict physical racial selection. The ideological indoctrination of the troops was seen as being as important as their military training. Aware of the fact that they were the Third Reich's elite, they showed exceptional courage, loyalty and absolute obedience to the Nazi state.

Those infantrymen, who after 1942 were designated Panzergrenadiers or armored grenadiers, formed the backbone of those infantry units assigned to accompany tanks or Panzer units.

These youths belong to the SS Hitlerjugend division and they fought ferociously. A few went as far as to commit war crimes against Canadian prisoners in war in reprisal, they alleged, for similar atrocities. (Bundesarchiv)

Because of the age of the unit's troops the Hitlerjugend was nicknamed the Baby Division by the British at the start of the campaign. The nickname was soon dropped. (Militaria Magazine)

This SS man, photographed in August 1944 as the Germans pulled back over the Seine, wears a grey-green fatigue cap first issued in 1940 and different to that issued to Army units. (© ECPAD/France)

Here at Rouen on August 25, 1944 this young SS corporal wears the classic campaign dress in grey-green, first manufactured in 1942-1943. (© ECPAD/France)

Such was the case in Normandy where the SS exclusively employed such infantry. One of the most famous such units was the 12th SS Panzer Division (Hitlerjugend).

Composed on the whole of young volunteers, with an average age of just 17, it was considered as being operational from June 1 1944, despite certain problems. The Hitlerjugend launched its first counter-attack on the afternoon of June 7, fighting Canadians around Caen. These young soldiers amazed their opponents by their tenacity, endurance and contempt for death.

They fought ferociously and prevented the Anglo-Canadians from reaching Caen on time. The unit was pulled back on June 11 in order to recuperate, having lost 4,485 men of which 1,000 had been killed. The unit's commander, SS-Brigadeführer Fritz Witt was killed on June 14 and replaced by SS-Standartenführer Kurt Meyer. The division was back in action by July 19 having being used to form two combat groups, Kampfgruppen Wünsche and Waldmüller.

These fought to the south of Caen and were used to counter *Operation Goodwood* and block the advance of British VIII Corps. Similarly, these units contributed to the failure of *Operation Totalize* on August 7, destroying nearly 200 Allied tanks in the coming days. On August 16, a group of around 50 men, dug in at a girls' high school in Falaise fought to the death. Isolated units helped keep the Falaise pocket open before breaking out themselves towards Trun and Chambois on August 20 and 21.

The division lost some 8,000 men during the course of the campaign and most of its heavy equipment too.

The P08 automatic pistol, a 9mm caliber handgun which was gradually replaced by the P38. (Private collection)

Top: This insignia was first issued in 1939 and was awarded to those wounded once or twice. There were two further classes of award, one silver and one gold. (Private collection)

Previous page: The eagle sleeve badge as issued to Waffen SS units. It differed from the Army badge which, in any case, was worn on the front of the tunic. (Private collection)

25

THE ARMY TANK-DESTROYER OFFICER

German tank-destroyer (Panzerjäger) and assault gun (Sturmgeschütze) units, the latter equipped with the Sturmgeschütze III or IV, played an important role in Normandy. Of all the German armor engaged in the campaign it notched up the best scores against Allied tanks.

This view is a close up of a Panzerjäger or Sturmgeschütze crewman. At the time of the Normandy campaign only the collar tabs were regulation issue (grey with red or pink piping) but older versions continued to persist. (© ECPAD/France)

The MP 40 submachine gun. Armor crews made considerable use of this weapon and it was frequently part of the equipment found on board. (Vincey Museum)

These assault gun units were subdivisions of the German artillery and were required to perform diverse tasks. As the conflict evolved they were increasingly pitched into battle against Allied tanks and, to that extent, differed little from the Panzerjägers. All divisions, whether they were infantry or Panzer units, had a battalion of tank destroyers attached to them. This was composed of four companies of which, for Panzer divisions or motorized infantry, only the first two were equipped with armored vehicles (14 each).

Assault gun units were deployed in brigades attached to the general reserve. Four such brigades fought in Normandy: the Sturmgeschütze-Brigaden 341 and 394, Sturmgeschütze-Abteilung 902 and Fallschirm-Sturmgeschütze-Brigade 12. Each had 31 StuG except the 341st which had 45. The 12th, which was actually stationed in Normandy on D-day, fought around Saint-Lô, Vire and Bayeux. It was a battle-hardened unit and fought well but it lost all of its vehicles, with the exception of just one assault gun, at Falaise. One of the unit's aces was Oberwachtmeister Grünwald who destroyed more than 20 enemy tanks. StuG Brigade 341 was sent up

Fatigue is written all over the faces of these men as they withdraw towards Falaise. The man on the left wears the old-style collar tabs issued specifically to motorized units. ((c)ECPAD/France)

A group of officers belonging to a self-propelled gun unit in Normandy. (© ECPAD/France)

A regulation compass of the type which first appeared in 1940. (Private collection)

from Narbonne to the Normandy front, arriving on July 31, at the Brécey-Avranches sector. It suffered so heavily that the butcher's bill at the end of the first day of fighting showed that the two batteries engaged had been almost entirely destroyed. Brought back up to strength it was pulled back slowly towards Brittany.

StuG Brigade 394 was quartered at Azay-le-Rideau on June 6 and had to wait until it was fully equipped before heading for the front. It reached La Flèche on August 1, before pushing on to Mortain. On August 4 it fought at Vire, distinguishing itself in the process. On August 6 one of its batteries was credited with the destruction of 26 Sherman tanks. The unit only managed to save one StuG from the Falaise debacle. The Allied landings took the StuG-Abteilung 902 by surprise at Tours.

It was soon in action in the Cotentin peninsula, near Valognes. Squeezed by the American offensive it withdrew westwards towards La-Haye-des-Puits. It managed to escape encirclement and only suffered light casualties until mid-July. By August 1 there were just a few vehicles belonging to the unit which were still operational.

The StuG Abteilung 1348, a very small formation, arrived in Normandy on August 6 but it is not clear where it was engaged.

This young officer wears a tunic of the type similar to that used by tank crews, although theirs was black, much used by personnel from motorized units. (Militaria Magazine)

THE LUFTWAFFE FIELD DIVISION JÄGER

The Luftwaffe's field divisions (Luftwaffenfelddivisionen) were created in 1942 at the instigation of Reichsmarschal Hermann Göring, commander in chief of the German air force. Used to bolster Germany's ground forces these troops were, towards the end of 1943, integrated into the Army but retained their original uniforms. Two such divisions fought in Normandy — the 16th and 17th.

Most of the troops used to create these units came from depots and so combat came as a rude shock to their morale. This situation was exacerbated by the fact that unit officers, many

A column of prisoners. When the 16th Field Division left Holland it had 9,816 men, 28 pieces of artillery and 32 anti-tank guns. (© ECPAD/France)

This soldiers displays one of the most distinctive characteristics of the Luftwaffe field divisions: the 1942 battledress. It was a simplified version of the type issued to the paratroopers. (Militaria Magazine)

of whom had little training in ground operations, were unfit to command infantry.

The baptism of fire for such soldiers led to heavy casualties in a relatively short space of time.

The 16th Division was part of the force tasked with occupying The Netherlands at the time of the Allied landings and was based around The Hague and Haarlem. It had no experience of combat and was practically without transport.

The bulk of the division was sent off to Normandy between June 16 and June 24 but most of the companies were undermanned and there was little artillery. Its first action of note was an encounter with British forces taking part in *Operation Charnwood*. It is most likely that the division deployed only one of its regiments in the sector to the east of the Orne and this was virtually destroyed, losing 75% of its effective strength.

Hill 64, held by the division, also came under attack. The German defenders lost 45% of their strength in just eight hours of fighting. This meant that the Anglo-Canadians were able to push on to their next objective — the bridges over the Orne.

During *Operation Goodwood* the 16th Field Division was in the German frontline, dug in between Colombelles and Troarn, and they suffered massive casualties. All the commanders of the regiments and the battalions were casualties as well as 36 company officers. The loss of most of its officers meant that the division effectively ceased to operate and its men were used to reinforce other units. By August 4 the division ceased to exist.

From early 1943 the 17th Field Division was in position on the coast between Fécamp and Le Havre. It was moved towards the front in early August and reached Dreux on the 17th.

It fought the Americans at Pacy-sur-Eure and on the August 25, pulled back to Louviers. Lost much of its artillery to Allied air raids and, after crossing the Seine, its personnel were integrated into the 331st Division.

Top: These Jäger of the 16th Field Division are armed with the redoubtable Panzerfaust and seem determined to await the enemy. Each anti-tank company included 18 Panzerschrecks. (© ECPAD/France)

Previous page: The use of helmet netting made it possible to attach leaves and branches to the helmet, something very common among the infantry. (Private collection)

Rouen, August 25, 1944. This soldier of the 17th Field Division has escaped the Falaise pocket and awaits further instructions. (© ECPAD/France)

A Luftwaffe badge issued to ground forces, instituted on March 31, 1942. (Militaria Magazine)

A field cap (Einheits-Feldmutze). Just as in the Army, this cap became standard issue to the Luftwaffe from mid-1943. (Private collection)

29

THE LUFTWAFFE FIGHTER PILOT

The exhausted Luftwaffe failed to make its presence felt in the skies above Normandy. Despite the fact that the Allied air force completely outnumbered the Germans (there was one German plane for every 50 Allied planes on June 6), the Luftwaffe had 1,300 airplanes in the west on June 10. Of these 474 were fighter aircraft.

At the time of the Allied landings there were just two German fighter squadrons present in the west: Jagdgeschwader 2 and Jagdgeschwader 26. As D-day drew to a close only a few Allied airplanes had fallen victim to these units. In the course of the campaign further squadrons were brought forward in support — Jagdgeschwaders 1, 3, 5, 11, 27, 53 and 54.

Most of the German aircraft involved in the campaign flew from around 100 airfields in either Brittany and the Pas de Calais. These were some distance from the combat zone, being some 60

These pilots are resting between missions. Captain Robert "Bazi" Weiss on the right unwinds. This ace notched up 121 victories but was killed in action on December 29, 1944. (© ECPAD/France)

....

This officer is equipped for flying and wears a LKp N 101 flying helmet. His leather jacket is a civilian item and was of the kind much prized by fighter pilots. The pilot's pants are grey-blue and lined with synthetic fur. (Militaria Magazine)

A group of pilots belonging to JG5 resting in France. Behind them is an Fw-190. Most German fighter pilots flew the Focke Wulf Fw-190A or the Messerschmitt Bf 109G over Normandy. (© ECPAD/France)

This JG1 pilot is in the cockpit of his Focke Wulf 190 and is adjusting his flying helmet. On August 20th the number of fighter aircraft present in the West reached 581. (© ECPAD/France)

miles on average from the Normandy coast. A few aircraft did fly from Normandy airfields such as Lonrai, Semallé, Essay, Marcilly and Saint-André-de-l'Eure. German fighter pilots, most of whom were very young but full of courage, fought odds of one against ten for three months. More than a thousand of them became casualties (killed, wounded or missing). Fighting against Mustangs, Thunderbolts, Typhoons and Spitfires, flown by pilots from well-equipped units, didn't give the Germans much hope of a successful outcome. Even so German fighters over Normandy were credited with 1,200 victories.

Among the aces who distinguished themselves over this front were Captain Siegfried *"Wumm"* Lemke and second-lieutenant Wilhelm Hofmann of JG26, who shot down 23 aircraft; Captain Theodor Weissenberger of JG5, credited with 25; Lieutenant Hans-Joachim Schliedermann of JG27, credited with seven; Adjutant Heinrich Bartels of JG27 who shot down 11; Lieutenant Paul Becker of JG27 with eight; Captain Emil Lang (JG54) the ace of aces over Normandy credited with 28 victories; and Captain Robert *"Bazi"* Weiss of JG54 with 18.

A Luftwaffe pilot's badge. Created in March 1936 it was issued to students who graduated from flying school at the same time that their flying licence was issued. (Militaria Magazine)

A wrist combat, type AK39. (JLF collection)

A Walther signal gun. A shot-down pilot would use this to signal his presence to friendly forces. (JLF collection)

31

Medics

First aid units and Army medical personnel played an important role on the battlefields of Normandy. They worked in difficult conditions but their intervention saved thousands of lives.

These men, given the mission of evacuating wounded in difficult circumstances, were part of an army on the defensive and consequently paid a heavy price in the course of their duty.

The military nurse was trained in a medical school and attached to company command. In combat he was assisted by soldiers who were trained to act as stretcher-bearers or by medics given rudimentary first aid training before being assigned to medical units.

The wounded were treated in the field and then sent back to battalion first-aid posts.

Then, depending upon the nature of the wound, they were sent to regimental hospitals or, if they were seriously wounded, were carried by stretcher and placed on an ambulance. These took them to divisional hospitals generally some ten miles behind the front.

These were established either in tents

Medical personnel often wore overalls wearing a large red cross to distinguish their function. (©ECPAD/France)

Right: A sleeve badge worn by privates and NCOs who had completed their medical training but were not officially medical personnel. (PS Collection)

The 1939 model nurse's backpack as worn on campaign. It contained spare dressings. (Militaria Magazine)

A group of soldiers have just come under attack from Allied fighter bombers. A nurse has been wounded. He is being tended by one of his comrades. Another medic, on the right, has fixed a white brassard to his helmet. (DR)

32

A *German ambulance in Lisieux. (©)ECPAD/France)*

B *rassard worn by a stretcher bearer. (Militaria Magazine)*

or in buildings and were staffed by doctors, surgeons and nurses and had excellent infrastructures.

The patients who were temporarily unfit for service or were permanently incapable of rejoining their units were frequently transferred by train to hospitals in the rear.

A *docket used to identify wounded due for evacuation. This version, with the red borders, was issued to seriously wounded soldiers who should only be moved in exceptional circumstances. (Private collection)*

T *his adjutant wears a uniform with insignia which announce his function. Apart from this helmet and brassard he also has two brownleather first-aid kits on his belt. These contained dressings, gauze, antiseptics, tweezers and scissors. His canteen is also specific to medical personnel and could carry up to 100 centiliters. (Militaria Magazine)*

33

PRACTICAL INFORMATION

In this section we have provided practical guidance on sites and museums of interest in Normandy. We have included details of the most representative sites and those located as close as possible to the actual events covered in this book. For those who want to see military vehicles we recommend the practical information sections of the books Armor in Normandy.

In Calvados

Five miles to the north of Caen, at Ouistreham, there is a **museum commemorating the landing of No. 4 Commando**. Uniforms, weapons and equipment are on display as well as documents relating to the landing of Anglo-French commandos at Sword Beach. The site is dedicated to the 177 commandos belonging to Kiefferís unit. Thereís also a monument alongside the D514, as it enters the south of the town, and another on the sea front.

○ *Musée du débarquement des commandos No 4*
Place Alfred-Thomas
14150 Ouistreham
Tel: 02 31 96 63 10

Further along the coast, 15 miles to the east, you arrive at Beneville-sur-Mer. Close by is **Mont Caisy**, transformed by the Germans into one of the most important batteries in the Atlantic Wall. There are numerous casemates, bunkers, observation posts and gun positions to visit as well as 20 miles of tunnels.

○ *Site de la batterie du Belvédère au Mont Caisy*
Les Amis du Mont Caisy
Mairie
14910 Beneville-sur-Mer
Tel: 02 31 87 92 64
Fax: 02 31 87 32 15

Opening hours: from April to September, Saturday and Sunday 14.30 to 17.30.There are free guided tours of the fortifications and installations which last 2 hours. These are given by volunteers of the Friends of Mont Caisy. There is car parking. Bring torches.

Turning back towards Bayeux, the **memorial museum to General de Gaulle** recalls the great man's visits to the city. It focuses on the visit of June 14, 1944 and that of June 16, 1946. There are numerous photos and documents on display and films are also shown.

○ *General de Gaulle Memorial Museum*
10 rue Bourbesneur
14400 Bayeux
Tel: 02 31 92 45 55
Opening hours: 15 March to 15 November, 09.30 ñ 12.30 and 14.00 to 18.30.

The largest British cemetery of World War II is to the south of Bayeux. It contains the graves of 4,648 Allied and German soldiers, of which 3,935 are British. Heading west along Route Nationale 13, the visitor will reach the vast La **Cambe cemetery**. Here 21,500 German soldiers lie buried beneath five huge black crosses. Thereís a memorial chapel at the entrance. Another **German cemetery** lies close by at Saint-Germain-du-Pert.

Five miles from there, on the coast, is the **Rangers Museum** at Grandcamp Maisy. It commemorates this elite American unit and its attack on Pointe-du-Hoc on D-Day.

○ *Rangers Museum*
Mairie
14450 Grandchamp-Maisy
Tel: 02 31 92 33 51

Heading along the D514 you reach Vierville-sur-Mer and the **museum for the Omaha** landings. It's an impressive collection of equipment, uniforms, artillery, weapons and even aircraft engines.

○ *Musée D-day d'Omaha*
Route de Grandchamp
14710 Vierville-sur-Mer
Tel: 02 31 21 71 80
Open between 30 March and 10 November.

Some three miles further down the D514 is Coleville-sur-Mer with its **American Cemetery**. It covers 20 hectares and there are more than 9,000 white crosses. Most of the soldiers buried here were killed during the landing. Thereís a memorial chapel to American youth.

Further inland, some twenty miles to the south west of Bayeux is a memorial museum dedicated to the fighting in bocage country.

○ *Musée de la Percée du Bocage*
14350 Saint-Martin-des-Besaces
Tel: 02 31 67 52 78

The **Friends of the Suffolk Regiment** organize visits and guided tours of the Hillman fortifications at Coleville-Montgomery, a German command post with 18 emplacements which was taken by the 1st battalion of the regiment on June 7, 1944.

○ *Friends of the Suffolk Regiment*
Mairie de Colleville-Montgomery
Tel: 02 31 97 12 61
www.amis-du-suffolk-rgt-com
Open every Tuesday until 15.00 in July and August. Tours last 1.30 hours.

In the La Manche Region

Passing into the La Manche region on the RN 13 you soon reach the Carentan canal and then Sainte-Marie-du-Mont with its **Utah Beach museum**. It is the only museum dedicated to the landings there in the entire region and the exhibits are first class. Allied assault equipment and German defensive equipment are presented and videos are shown in three languages. There's a panoramic view over Utah Beach itself and Pointe-du-Hoc.

○ *Utah Beach Museum*
50480 Sainte-Marie-du-Mont
Tel: 02 33 71 53 35

Opening hours: from 15 March to 15 November, 10.00 to 12.30 and 14.00 to 17.30.

Another fascinating site is 10 miles to the north-west at Crisbecq. It's the **German battery of Azeville and Saint-Marcouf**. There were four casemates here, armed with 105 mm artillery and eight blockhouses with a garrison of 170 artillerymen. There is